SO-AAE-017

Advance praise for
The Child with Autism Learns about Faith

"Just when you thought Kathy Labosh's *The Child with Autism* series couldn't get any better, along comes another remarkable book for parents and educators of children with autism: *The Child with Autism Learns about Faith* is a comprehensive, step-by-step guide to enriching the lives of children through religious education. Using a Judeo-Christian model as her foundation, Labosh presents biblical stories in meaningful, bite-size segments that children of all ages and abilities can relate to. Creative hands-on activities, catchy songs and memorable daily prayers complement each lively lesson.

Besides serving as a testament to Labosh's education and sensitivity, the author's incorporation of Jewish references and Hebrew terminology makes *The Child with Autism Learns about Faith* appealing to members of the Jewish community at large. It is an indispensable reference tool for any parent and/or educator who believes in the timeless values, lessons, and mores inherent in religious history and practice. Kudos to Labosh for filling such a vital need within the exceptional community."

— Aviva Engel, Editor, *Exceptional Family*

"The book's easy-to-use lessons and multi-sensory approach are just right for teaching children with ASD. The practical tips will help congregations engage all children with opportunities to grow in faith. The lessons can be adjusted to accommodate varying degrees of cognitive abilities. The contemplative questions for parents and caregivers are a wonderful guide that can facilitate fellowship and help family members express underlying sentiments that often remain unspoken. ... this book is an essential tool for every faith community that wants to provide meaningful participation to all its members."

— Sister Kathleen Schipani, IHM, and Mrs. Lori Brew
The Department for Pastoral Care for Persons with Disabilities
Archdiocese of Philadelphia

"I happily recommend this book, *The Child with Autism Learns about Faith*. The author faithfully and creatively presents the early stories of the Sacred Scripture using teaching methods that help children with autism learn the Biblical stories and their message for today. It is so vitally important that we have good and effective catechetical resources for children with disabilities. I am deeply grateful for Kathy Labosh's service to the Church in writing this excellent book to assist teachers and parents in sharing the faith with children with autism."

— The Most Reverend Kevin C. Rhoades,
Bishop of Fort Wayne-South Bend, Indiana

the Child with Autism

Learns about Faith

15 ready-to-use scripture lessons,
from the Garden of Eden
to the parting of the Red Sea

KATHY LABOSH

FUTURE HORIZONS INC.
Arlington, Texas

 **Learns about Faith**

All marketing and publishing rights guaranteed to and reserved by:

FUTURE HORIZONS INC.

721 W. Abram Street
Arlington, Texas 76013
800-489-0727
817-277-0727
817-277-2270 (fax)
E-MAIL: *info@FHautism.com*
www.FHautism.com

© 2011 Kathy Labosh

Book design © TLC Graphics, *www.TLCGraphics.com*
Cover by: Monica Thomas; Interior by: Erin Stark

All rights reserved.

No part of this book may be reproduced in any manner whatsoever without written permission of Future Horizons, Inc., except in the case of brief quotations embodied in reviews.

Unless otherwise noted, all scripture readings come from The New American Bible, © 1957 World Bible Publishers. Revised 1991.

Disclaimer: Please note that the materials contained in this book are based on the author's own experience and/or information obtained by the author from other sources. This book is for informational purposes only. The reader is advised to use his or her best judgment in applying the information to the reader's own situation and care of his or her children. This book cannot be construed as providing any medical, health, legal, child, or product safety advice. All company and product names, logos, and trademarks included in the book are exclusive property of their respective holders.

Publisher's Cataloging-In-Publication Data
(Prepared by The Donohue Group, Inc.)

Labosh, Kathy.
   The child with autism learns about faith / Kathy Labosh.
      p. ; cm. – (The child with autism)
   "15 ready-to-use scripture lessons, from the Garden of Eden to the parting of the Red Sea."
   Includes bibliographical references and index.
   ISBN: 978-1-935274-19-3
   1. Autistic children—Education—Religious aspects. 2. Christian education of children with mental disabilities. I. Title.
RJ506.A9 L23 2011
649/.154

Printed in the United States of America

Nihil Obstat
Given at Harrisburg, PA on the 20th of October, 2006
by Carol L. Houghton, STD, JCD, Censor librorum.

Imprimatur
Given at Harrisburg, PA on the 20th of October, 2006
by The Most Reverend Kevin C. Rhoades, Bishop of Harrisburg.

The nihil obstat and imprimatur are declarations
that a book or pamphlet is free of doctrinal or moral error.
No implication is contained therein that those who have
granted the nihil obstat or imprimatur agree
with the contents, opinions, or statements expressed.

This book is dedicated to Rev. Joseph Celia
1940–2005
He loved the flock and the flock loved him.

Table of Contents

Foreword

In October 2005, Kathy Labosh presented a remarkable workshop to parishioners and parish staff of the Archdiocese of Philadelphia on partnering in religious education for children with autism spectrum disorders (ASD). Her engaging and humorous style expressed and validated many of the experiences of those workshop participants who were raising a child with ASD. It provided others with a glimpse into the lives of families who, every day, must navigate through an environment that is not always sensitive to children with ASD.

As members of faith communities we must welcome all members of God's family. To do so, we need greater understanding of all who come to fellowship with us, and we must provide opportunities for each person's meaningful participation. Faith communities should strive to support the blessings and challenges of raising children of all abilities.

All people are designed for spiritual connectedness. Ensuring that individuals with ASD are fully integrated into their faith community is not only important to the individual and family, but also to the faith community. It provides the congregation with a true representation of the diversity of all members of society and reflects a more accurate portrayal of individuals living with disabilities. With the compassionate understanding and increased knowledge found in *The Child with Autism Learns about Faith,* we are confident that faith communities will inflict fewer painful experiences like the one Ms. Labosh shares in this book's opening pages. The book's easy-to-use lessons and multi-sensory approach are just right for teaching children with ASD. The practical tips will help congregations engage all children with opportunities to grow in faith. The lessons can be adjusted to accommodate varying degrees of cognitive abilities. The contemplative questions for parents and caregivers are a wonderful guide that can facilitate fellowship and help family members express underlying sentiments that often remain unspoken.

Ms. Labosh's initiative in developing this book is a testament to her own dedication and commitment to the Christian faith. We commend her efforts to help faith communities incorporate all their members into the full life of fellowship. *The Child with Autism Learns about Faith* will inspire, encourage, and assist all those who share that priority. Statistics suggest ASD occurs in 1:110 children; surely this book is an essential tool for every faith community that wants to provide meaningful participation to all its members.

SISTER KATHLEEN SCHIPANI, IHM
MRS. LORI BREW
The Department for Pastoral Care
for Persons with Disabilities
Archdiocese of Philadelphia

Preface

In 1994, my family visited a beautiful old cathedral while we were on vacation. Sam began babbling during the service and an usher came up and motioned for us to follow. I thought he would lead us to a cry room, but instead we were escorted outside. The sound of those heavy doors closing behind us is unforgettable.

I knew God was not rejecting us—only the usher was—but the pain went deep, nevertheless. Others might have left the church for good after an experience like that. Fortunately, it wasn't my home church, and I loved God and my faith too much to leave.

I am very proud of my home diocese of Harrisburg. They started an outreach group for families of children with developmental disabilities—St. Raphael's Outreach, named for the archangel whose name means "God Heals." At one meeting I listened to other parents talk about how hurt they felt when their children were turned down for religious education. The families felt isolated and abandoned by their church. My frustration and empathy turned into a sense of purpose—to get a religious education class started for the children in our church who have developmental disabilities.

My first step was to approach the Director of Religious Education (DRE) about the need for a special education classroom. She said, "Great. I'll find you a room; just tell me what you need." I should have seen that coming, but I had not.

Courage is doing something even if you're scared, just because it needs to be done. I was terrified at the thought of leading the religious education of the developmentally disabled, so I can empathize with DREs and teachers everywhere. Even with my knowledge of autism, I still felt overwhelmed. How scared and lost others must feel when they are dealing with an unfamiliar disability.

The class got started during the Christmas season, so my first class was called "Happy Birthday Jesus." I brought decorations, a cake, and small presents for the children. At the beginning of the class, I suddenly realized that I had forgotten the candles for the cake. As if on cue, someone from the church brought me a small candle with a picture of the nativity on the side. It was a thank-you gift for my organizing the class. It was also the perfect candle for the cake! At that point, I felt that God was blessing my project, and knew that He would make up for my weaknesses.

That first year was both trying and exhilarating. There were days when I felt like the ringmaster in a circus gone awry. But even on those days, I saw God touching the children and the parents in unexpected ways. All God wanted from me was a willingness to reach out. We pray for God's help and we get it in abundance, because He wants our help in reaching these kids and families. God will help you; He will be there for you as He was for me. He loves these children immensely. With this book, you will be able to benefit from my experiences. Have courage, and God bless.

KATHY LABOSH

Part One

Class Preparation

The Why, Who, When, & What

Part one includes information on the importance of developing ministry targeted to the autistic population and how to prepare for teaching them. You will learn:

The Importance of Outreach

How They Learn

Classroom Setup

Material & Resources

Chapter 1

The Importance of Outreach

Many people are familiar with the parable of the ninety-nine sheep. The Good Shepherd has one hundred sheep, and when he loses one of them, he leaves the ninety-nine sheep to find the one that was lost. Well, I am going to tell you a parable of the stressed shepherd.

> There once was a shepherd who had one hundred sheep. When one of them was missing, he *knew* it was the one with the black spot on his tail. He just was not like the other sheep. Sheep naturally follow other sheep; the stressed shepherd figured this one must be deaf, or he must be a loner. He did not seem to want to be near the other sheep.
>
> So the next time the sheep with the black spot was missing, the stressed shepherd searched for a while, and then returned to his flock. After all, he had ninety-nine other sheep to look out for. This one lamb was more work than all the rest put together, and it just was not right to neglect the ninety-nine to look for a lamb that did not want to be a part of the flock anyway. This decision saddened him, but he also felt somewhat relieved.
>
> Some months later, there was a severe drought, and all the shepherd's usual sources of water had dried up.

The sheep were struggling to survive, and so was he. The shepherd cried out to God for help, and when he looked up, he saw a fat sheep standing on a hilltop. The shepherd followed the sheep into a canyon, where cool, clear water was springing from a rock, and a lot of green vegetation was flourishing all around the spring.

As the shepherd thanked God for rescuing him and his flock, he noticed that the fat sheep had a black spot on his tail! He wept when he realized that, if he had only taken the time to rescue that sheep, he would have found the spring before the drought had even begun. He and his flock would have had a source of strength to help them survive the drought.

The moral of the story is that we need every person to be complete. Those who challenge us the most can bring out the best in us. When people see what someone with disabilities is up against, their own burden seems lighter. They resolve to try a little harder. Children who are ill elicit more compassion and patience from us than do a hundred sermons. They are God's powerful agents of change in the world today.

However, there are many challenges, and the families of children with developmental disabilities need the love and understanding of their faith communities. Families often are unable to bring their children with disabilities to regular church functions because of a child's anxiety or behavior issues. They can feel judged by others who think autism is a discipline problem. Many marriages are tested by the strain. These families need to hear that God loves them, and that His people are here to support them. Unfortunately, their isolation makes them nearly invisible to those around them, and they often suffer alone.

If your heart is ready to reach out to these families, this book will tell you how to accomplish that. You and your faith commu-

nity will find blessings and strengths that will carry you through the hardest times. Be encouraged by this Scripture:

The learned will shine as brightly as the vault of heaven, and those who have instructed many in virtue as bright as stars for all eternity (Daniel 12:3; Jerusalem Bible).

Chapter 2

How They Learn

Before you can begin to teach a child with autism, you need to understand how autism affects the ability to process information. You will understand why most traditional methods don't work for these children. But most importantly, you will learn simple teaching methods that *do* reach children with autism.

Autism is a physical disability of the brain. Just as blindness affects the eye, and deafness affects the ear, autism affects the brain. Autopsies of people with autism have shown that some of their brain cells are small and immature, as if they were waiting for the signal to develop.

Other parts of the brain are over-developed, but only a few thin filaments connect one part of the brain to another. Although the problem is physical, the effects are often behavioral. So the first thing teachers and others who work with children with autism must understand is that autism is a disease. It cannot be "disciplined away."

Children with autism have difficulty processing information. For example, typical children's books have many intricate pictures, fanciful characters, and rich language meant to stimulate a child's imagination. This works well for typical children, but spells trouble for the child with autism.

Let me use this example to highlight how the autistic mind works. Intricate pictures work against children with autism. Everything on the page is seen as equivalent—no special importance is attached to any one character or object. They might find the number of bricks in a wall just as interesting (or even more interesting) as the characters in the story.

Because they take in everything equally and at once, they should be introduced slowly to new environments, and given time to explore. After they have mapped out everything in their head, whenever they enter a room they will notice only what is different. So, whether you're working with a picture from a book or an object in a room, you need to let students with autism know which objects are significant to what you're teaching.

If you are reading a book out loud, they might have problems understanding you. They often have trouble distinguishing consonants; *cat, bat, mat, fat,* and *rat* can sound similar to them. To compensate for this deficiency, they tend to look at the speaker's mouth to lip-read. Unfortunately, they then miss the expression in the speaker's eyes, which can transmit a lot of information. You need to speak slowly, and enunciate clearly when you speak. Let your students see your face in case they need to lip-read.

Individuals with autism can also have trouble understanding you if you are speaking in a noisy room. Typical people can focus in on one sound and filter out background noise; individuals with autism cannot. All noise is interpreted equally. The noisier the room, the less they will understand—and the more agitated they will become. Cut down on background noise as much as possible, especially if the students are even a little bit stressed. You are teaching them important information, and you want them to get it correctly.

Children with autism take everything literally. If there are fairies in the story, then fairies exist. They will not understand why you would tell them something that is not true. If you are reading them a fictional story, then tell them it is "pretend" before you start. When you present stories from the Bible, stick to the story. Their simple faith is a beautiful gift. The parts of the brain that are involved in higher reasoning are physically impaired. Reasoning with individuals with autism is usually an exercise in frustration. Keep it simple, or you risk losing credibility.

Watch what you teach and read to them. They will believe what you say—that is, if they can understand you. Autism affects language comprehension. The biggest problem a child with autism faces when reading a book is the rich language. Single words are understood best, followed by simple sentences of two or three words. The higher the level of vocabulary and sentence structure, the less they will understand. Most religious education classes and regular classes are taught with textbooks and lectures. So when children with autism are taught alongside other children, just about everything goes over their heads. They usually get in trouble by trying to occupy their time until the class ends. Just remember that the more you read and the more you speak, the less they will understand.

This may leave you wondering what methods of communication are left to you. Well, have you ever had a dream? In dreams, we think in pictures, and this is just what individuals with autism do. Most think in pictures instead of words. Individuals with autism process information about the world around them through physical interaction with it and by studying what they see. Thoughts run through their minds as a stream of images, like a video. They often communicate by bringing a person to what they want so the person can see it.

If you want to bring children with autism to knowledge of your faith, you need to use images as well as physical interaction with the objects they are studying. The lesson plans in this book are designed to reach the children this way. The spoken word is used only to supplement the pictures and other activities.

This may sound complicated, but it's not. In fact, it is an ancient way of passing on the faith. The walls of the catacombs of Rome are covered with pictures of Scripture stories. Even today, if you look at the pictures, you will be able to identify which stories are being told. Be encouraged! It is possible to bring these children to an understanding of the stories that have transmitted our faith across millennia!

Our forebearers fought many obstacles to bring faith to our generation. We need to join together to bring it to those with autism in the next generation. They deserve to be a part of the great sweep of religious history, too.

Chapter 3

The Classroom Setup

The ideal religious education or Sunday school class for children with autism would be led by a teacher who is experienced in special education, and would include an aide for each child. There would be a separate table for each child and his aide to work on. The parents could be in a separate room, getting a break from their kids and working on their own Bible study.

The problem is that the dream classroom can be nearly impossible to set up and nightmarish to maintain. Special education professionals are often too tired from their regular jobs to want to lead another special education class. Teenagers make great aides—until some sport or other activity interferes. You need a long list of volunteers. I have found that the best solution is to have the parents work with their child or another child. During that time, the parents can often discuss things that are going on their lives and bond with each other. It is easier to get an aide or two to fill in if needed than to get numerous aides to commit to months of classes. If things are different in your church or synagogue, I applaud your congregation.

Before the classes start, it's important to meet with all the parents to discuss each child's ability to comprehend language, their skill levels, and their behavior issues. You should also discuss goals for the year. Do the parents want their children to learn the Hebrew alphabet? Do they want their children to prepare for First Holy Communion? Are some of the parents simply interested in helping their children be more comfortable going into the church building? These goals can be worked on during "packet time," which we will discuss shortly.

Meeting with the parents will also help determine whether some children can be mainstreamed into a regular classroom with just a few minor adjustments. If a child can be mainstreamed, you and the parents should go over the regular lesson plan and highlight the facts you want the child to know. Once those decisions are made, a series of "fact cards" can easily be made, tailored to that child's needs. Each fact should be divided between two cards that the child must match in order to get the whole fact. For instance, "The two forms of the Eucharist" could be on one card, and "bread and wine" would be on the other card. Make up several fact cards for the child. He or she can work on matching facts while the other children are reading or listening to lectures. In this way, the mainstreamed child will receive the same information as the other children, only less of it. The mainstreamed child could have an aide redirect his attention when necessary, or help him with any crafts. Keep in mind that fine motor skills are often difficult for children with autism.

For children who are too young for the religious education class, I suggest you write a social story about going to church or synagogue. Use photographs of the interiors of the buildings. You can turn the photos into flashcards that the parents can use for matching. In this way, they can teach their children the names of the objects; they can also tell a social story of what goes on during a service. Parents can use this until their child is old enough to attend a class.

A child who does not have the cognitive or social skills necessary to be incorporated into a regular classroom is perfect for the disabilities class. These classes are structured to go through a series of individual and group activities. Each activity has a purpose, but activities can be added or deleted to suit your situation. Not every activity is going to reach each child, but everyone should be able to come away with something. Let's look at the order of activities, and then we can take a closer look at some of them.

- Opening prayer (group)
- Circle Time (group)
- Scripture reading (individually with aide)
- Packet time (individually with aide)
- Group activity (group)
- Video or music (group)
- Closing prayer (group)

The classes start with an opening prayer, which should be an important one in your faith. Possible prayers could be the Our Father, Hail Mary, Modeh Ani, or Shema Yisrael. Whatever prayer you choose should be repeated at the beginning of every class. Children with autism learn by repetition, and it won't be long until they are saying the prayer with you.

Another purpose of the opening prayer is to announce the start of class. The children and their aides should gather for Circle Time. This talk should be short, related to the story, and pertinent to issues in their lives. I have provided Circle-Time talks for each lesson.

After Circle Time, the children will go with their aides for Scripture reading: Each child will read or be read to from an ability-appropriate Bible. These Bibles can range from a felt picture Bible to a study Bible with photographs of the places and artifacts. A list of Bibles is included in Part One, Section D. When the Scripture reading is finished, the children and their aides will work on the individual activities found in their packets.

Packet time is the most important part of the class. Everyone is collectively taught one lesson, but each child has an aide (usually a parent), and individual work projects that match the skill and comprehension level of the child. These projects can include taking a tour of the house of worship, matching pictures, doing puzzles, coloring pictures, reading books, making crafts, and learning Hebrew letters. Packet time is devoted to working on the yearly goal set for the child.

Group activity follows packet time, and it should be a fun activity for the kids—one that enables them to physically interact with the story in some fashion. Some kids will need a lot of help; others will not. Let the child choose his own comfort level, and do not force him to participate.

Chapter 6 lists many thematically relevant story videos. *Veggie Tales* or other wholesome videos would be fine, too.

The kids love songs. If your congregation has musicians who would be willing to share their talents with the children, they would find a very receptive audience. Of course, you could also play CDs or a kids' music video. You'll find some good options in Chapter 6.

The class ends with a closing prayer, which sums up a response to what the children have learned about God through that lesson. The closing prayer also signals to the children that the class is over.

The class is designed to be flexible. Feel free to add or delete sections to fit your needs and time constraints. The parents' Scripture study, which accompanies each lesson, is optional, but highly recommended. Parenting children with autism can feel isolating. It's good for parents to meet others in similar situations; it lets them realize that they are not alone in their experiences. Scripture study and discussion time provide opportunities for a life-affirming community to form.

Parents should do their reading ahead of class, but just reading the selected Scripture with a general knowledge of the story is sufficient for discussion. Parents should come prepared to discuss the questions. They can do that while their kids are watching a video, or among themselves while working with their kids. If you choose the latter option, be careful what you say—it's best not to discuss the negative aspects of dealing with autism. Like all children, those with autism will often understand more than you think they do.

This class is designed to meet the needs of children with autism *and* their parents. Most importantly, it is designed to pass faith on from one generation to the next, in ways that meet the special needs of this population. Before you get started, the task may seem like a massive undertaking, but it truly is not. Once you start working with the lessons, you will discover that you *can* do what God has asked of you. Best yet, the kids will learn that they are an important and valuable part of your faith community.

Chapter 4

The Materials

The best place to find materials is among your own *congregation*. They will have books, videos, toys, and puzzles lurking in their basements, attics, and playrooms. They don't want to keep them, but they don't want to throw them out, either. People want their things to go to good use. Giving them to special needs children is a blessing for them and for you.

Of course, a wealth of new publications, videos, and toys are available in bookstores and on the internet. In this chapter, I'm going to introduce you to some of these products. You'll find the information in the class segment where it will be used.

Materials Needed for Circle Time and Group Projects

A complete list of materials needed is included with each lesson in Part Two. The list here provides an overall picture of items you will probably need to purchase or borrow. You can use this list to ask your congregation to pitch in. Items that you are likely to have around the house or yard (for example, a flashlight or some rocks), or that can be easily and inexpensively purchased (fruit, crepe paper), are not included on this list.

- Terrarium kit (lesson 1)
- A variety of small stuffed animals (lessons 2 & 3)
- Baby name book (lesson 3)
- Noah's Ark toy (Lesson 6)
- Striped, multi-colored robe (lesson 10)
- Cloth tunnels (lesson 11)
- Large cardboard boxes (lesson 11)
- Plastic eggs (lesson 12)
- Finger puppets of the ten plagues— available from *www.oytoys.com* (lesson 14)
- Certificates and awards (lesson 15)

Chapter 5

Scripture Reading

Bibles for children should be based on their abilities. Basically, any Bible the child enjoys is fine, but there are some that I particularly like. For a child who is nonverbal, or who has very limited language, I recommend *The Beginner's Bible, Bible Beginnings-Book 1.* This felt Bible is produced by Little Folk Visuals. It covers most, but not all, of the stories in this Bible study. The other stories can be covered by buying additional felt pieces. Little Folk Visuals also publishes a *Bible in Felt Teacher's Manual* (copyright 1966, revised 1992).

For the child with some language, I recommend *Everyday Bible Stories* by Our Sunday Visitor, illustrated by Anna C. Lepler. This book is wonderful because the stories are short (none are longer than a page). There are 365 stories, which take you all the way through the Bible. You can always read more than one page if you want to. The only downside is that the pages have a date at the top, which probably will not correspond to the day you are reading it. That feature will bother some children with autism.

For older students who don't want anything "childish," I love *The Children's Illustrated Bible Stories,* retold by Selina Hasting and illustrated by Eric Thomas (DK Publishing, Inc., 1994). It has fantastic photographs of the biblical area, as well as maps, and pictures of artifacts. It still presents the story visually, but respects the student's age and maturity. The language level is okay, too—especially the language accompanying the photos.

DK Publishing also puts out *A First Book of Jewish Bible Stories.* I haven't seen it, so I don't know if it covers all the stories this lesson plan does.

Many of the children may already have a Bible appropriate to their abilities. This should be ascertained during the meeting with the parents before the classes start.

For the parents' Scripture study, I think a variety of Bible versions can add to the Bible study. But whatever Bible people already have is surely sufficient. We do not want the classes to become burdensome to the families by requiring things that are not truly needed.

Chapter 6

Packet
Time

Packets must be developed that are appropriate to each child's abilities and goals. A packet should be assembled for each child to work with individually, along with her aide. The work can mirror skills that she is currently working on in school, or has already mastered. It isn't difficult to put the packets together. Once you have the contents set, it's often just a case of updating the coloring picture and rotating the puzzles for each new lesson.

A low-functioning child may simply be matching pictures of animals, fruit, holy cards, or pictures of objects in your church or synagogue. Their packets can also include coloring pages related to the story. Simple puzzles are another good option. Listening to the aide read stories is another possibility for packet time.

A more advanced child may be doing connect-the-dot puzzles and other higher-level puzzles, reading stories, and playing card games.

A child who uses sign language could be learning Bible verses in sign. A Jewish child could be learning his Aleph Bet. A Catholic child could be preparing for his First Holy Communion.

There are some great websites and catalogs with wonderful selections of children's toys and activities. Many of these are also available in local religious bookstores. The following list is just a launching pad to give you an idea of what is out there and where you might find it. Once you start looking, you won't believe the variety of what's available!

www.oytoys.com For all things Jewish! Get puzzles and other activities to teach children the Aleph Bet. Also of interest at this website are:

- *Tasty Bible Stories*—a menu of tales and matching recipes by Tami Lehman-Wilzig, illustrated by Katherine Janus Kahn (Kar-Ben Publishing, 2003)
- *Bible Story Crafts for Little Hands* by Ruth Esrig Brinn, illustrated by Sally Springer (Kar-Ben Publishing, 2000). (I particularly like the Rachel's bracelets.)
- *In the Beginning*—a cloth activity book
- Creation Floor Puzzle (27 pieces)
- Noah's Ark Floor Puzzle (24 pieces)
- Noah's Ark Shape Sorter
- Noah Soft Playset
- Noah's Ark Animal Match
- Noah's Ark Sticker Stories
- Passover Ten Plagues Finger Puppets (lesson 14)

The Autom Catalog at www.autom.com has a variety of books to prepare children to receive the sacraments. Items of more general interest are:

- Fun with Bible Friends Coloring Book
- Fun with Bible Heroes Coloring Book
- Noah and the Flood Puzzle Book by St. Joseph Puzzle Books. It has five 12-piece puzzles that correspond to the story on the opposite page.

- Religious Fun and Game Book (assorted in pack—will contain Old and New Testament games)
- Bible Bingo Game (mix of Old and New Testament games)
- The *Hi God* CD collection
- Various children's Bibles

Pauline Books and Media at www.pauline.org carries:

- *The Bible for Little Ones* translated by Mary Nazarene Prestofillipo, FSP. This is a board book.
- Bible Stories—Find-the-Picture puzzles

Sadlier at www.sadlier.com has some wonderful large books that are terrific if you want to read in front of the children.

- *The Pre Primary 1*—includes Abraham, Moses, Samuel, David and Goliath.
- *The Pre-Primary 2*—includes Daniel, Jonah, Zacchaeus, the Little Lost Sheep
- *The Primary 1*—includes Elijah and the Big Showdown, Esther, Ruth, Joseph: The Favorite Son
- *The Primary 2*—Includes Jesus is with Us, Jesus' Miracles, Paul and Silas Go to Jail, Saul's Surprise on the Road to Damascus
- Sadlier also carries a Bible Felt Art Kit—pre-K-3

Carson-Dellosa Publishing at www.carsondellosa.com

- Bible Story Puppets and Poems
- Interactive Bible Story Bulletin Boards
- Easy Christian Crafts
- Play and Learn Bible Games
- The Good Book Cookbook
- Signs of Wisdom—Expressing God's Wisdom in Sign Language

- Faith Speaks—Expressing God's Word in Sign Language
- Name that Bible Character!—Puzzles and Clues from The Greatest Stories Ever Told
- Dot-to-Dot Bible Pictures
- Hidden Pictures
- Bible Story Puzzles

Harcourt Religion Publishers at www. harcourtreligion.com

- The Bible Big Books including *Abraham, God Made Our World, Joseph, the Favorite Son, Moses,* and *Noah*. These may be purchased separately instead of in sets.
- *Pray and Play Bible for Young Children*
- *Pray and Play Bible 2 for Young Children*
- Pray and Play Songs for Young Children

Catholic Child at www.catholicchild.com

- *Touch and Feel Bible Stories*
- *Lift the Flap Catholic Bible*
- *Lift and Look Creation* and *Noah's Ark* book set
- *Lift and Learn Old Testament Stories*
- Noah's Animal Alphabet Puzzle
- Noah's Ark Playmobil Set
- Noah's Rainbow Race Game
- CDs and DVDs for children

Standard Publishing at www.standardpub.com

- Thru-the-Bible Reproducible coloring book, illustrated by Janet Skiles. This is good for all the lessons.
- Bible Memory Game

Cook Communication Ministries of Canada at www.cook.ca carries some of my favorites:

• Bible Bingo
• Bible Old Man (plays like Old Man using Bible characters)
• Jonah, Go Fish Card Game
• Noah's Memory Match Up
• Bible Dominoes
• Who Do You See? (Plays like Where's Waldo?)

www.christian book.com—more resources than you'll ever need are available from this internet retailer.

Videos and Songs

Videos

Finding quality videos and DVDs for teenagers can be tricky. You definitely want to stay away from the cute cartoons. Teens want to be treated with respect for their age. I recommend The Bible Collection series put out by Turner Home Entertainment. They use famous actors and are generally very good. The video on creation may be a little boring for the kids and hard to follow. The other videos in the series are great—just take Genesis a little at a time. The series covers Genesis, Abraham, Jacob, Joseph, Moses, Samson and Delilah, David, Solomon, Esther, Paul the Apostle, and the Apocalypse.

The Bible in Animation series is good for elementary school kids. The series covers Creation and the Flood, Abraham, Joseph, Moses, Ruth, David and Saul, Elijah, Daniel, and Jonah.

For young children there are so many options: *Veggie Tales,* the *Cherub Wings, the Wemmicks*, and countless others.

You can find these videos and more at www.christiancinema.com and www.christianbook.com.

Songs

Children with autism remember words that they hear in song better than words that are spoken to them. If you can incorporate songs into your program, it could be very beneficial. Here is a list of songs (without copyright restrictions) that you may wish to incorporate.

- Adam was a Gardener
- Father Abraham
- Hava Nagila
- He's Got the Whole World in His Hands
- If You Are Happy and You Know It
- Jesus Loves Me
- Rise and Shine (The Arky, Arky Song)
- This Little Light of Mine

The words and tunes to these and other songs can be found at www.kididdles.com.

Numerous collections of worship songs and faith songs are available on CD from internet retailers and your local religious bookstore. Probably some members of your congregation will have some they are willing to share or donate.

The fifteen lessons included in this book require a variety of materials, but many are durable and can be used again and again. Videos, CDs, Bibles, and toys can serve through many terms. Don't forget: people want to help out by supplying resources. Ask the congregation. Much of what you need, you will find right there. Look for items that can be legally reproduced to include in the packets, as well as durable puzzles and card games that can be rotated among the children's packets throughout the term.

Part 2

Faith Lessons
for the Child with Autism

Creation
Adam Names the Animals
Adam and Eve
Temptation
Cain and Abel
Noah
Abraham
Isaac and Rebekah
Jacob
Joseph and His Dreams
Joseph in Egypt
Moses in the Bulrushes
Moses and the Burning Bush
Moses and Pharaoh
Passover and the Red Sea

Chapter 7

Creation

God Made Everything

Materials and Preparation

- Flashlight
- Water
- Rocks
- Plant
- Piece of fruit
- Stuffed animals
- Doll
- Terrarium kit(s)

Some of these items can be reused during the group project if you opt to do the terrarium project. For the terrarium project, you can buy a plastic terrarium at a pet store, as well as dirt and plants and other material to add to it. If someone has a small pet they would like to lend to the project, the animal can be added last, to represent the animals God made. (*Note*: Rabbits, for some unknown reason, have been known to terrify some children.)

Packets for the individual packet work should be prepared before the semester begins, according to the goals set for the individual students. Make sure the packets are ready before the first class. Choose an appropriate video, DVD, or CD to use during the lesson.

Lesson Objective

To help the children understand that God made everything in nature.

Opening Prayer

The same opening prayer is prayed at the start of every lesson.

Circle Time

Look around you and you see lots of things. But once there was a time when there was absolutely nothing except God. Do you know what the first thing He made was? Light (turn on the flashlight). Yup. Light! I guess He wanted to see. But He didn't make a flashlight. Man made that. God did make the sun and all the stars at night. Then He made the water. (Hold up the glass.) Then He made the earth that we are standing on. (Hold up the rock.) God made this. Next He made plants so that they would look beautiful (hold up plant), and so there would be food for His creatures to eat and air for them to breathe. Then He made all the birds, fish, and animals. (Hold up stuffed animals.)

God loved all the things He had made, but He wanted one more thing: someone to love. So he made people (hold up doll). He called the first man Adam.

Scripture Reading

Each aide should read the creation story to his or her student from an ability-appropriate Bible.

Packet Work

It's time for the kids to work individually (with their aide) on the goal-oriented work provided in the packet.

Group Activity

Use the terrarium kit to have the children make their own world by putting in dirt, rocks, and plants. Add water if plants are real.

Video/Songs

Choose a thematically appropriate video, DVD, or selection of songs to play. During this time, the parents can meet for their Scripture study.

Closing Prayer

God, thank you for the air I breathe and the food I eat. Thank you for making me.

PARENT'S SCRIPTURE STUDY

Individual Reading

Read Genesis 1:1-2:4

Selected Scripture

"In the beginning, when God created the heavens and the earth, the earth was a formless wasteland, and darkness covered the abyss, while a mighty wind swept over the waters.

Then God said, 'let there be light,' and there was light. God saw how good the light was. Then God separated the light from the darkness. God called the light 'day' and darkness he called 'night.' Thus evening came and morning followed—the first day."

Genesis 1:1-5

Contemplation

When most people want to explain the creation story and the wonders of God to children, they usually start with all the wonderful plants and animals he created. However, the first thing God created was order, a schedule we can plan our lives around.

Children with autism crave order and schedules. One way of introducing them to the awesome power of God might be to set up God's schedule for the day. Find out what times the sun and the moon will rise and set. Learn when the moon will be full, and the tides high. Show them that God made a schedule that our world and the universe follow.

Discussion Questions

- How does God's creation speak to you?
- Is there a way you can share that experience with your child?
- How might God's creation speak most powerfully to your child?

Chapter 8

Adam Names the Animals

God Has a Job For Us

Materials and Preparation

- Several small stuffed animals
- Index cards with animal names written on them to match the stuffed animals
- You will need a variety of small stuffed animals for the children to name. These will be used later for the zoo.
- Rotate packet items and add new items as necessary.
- Choose an appropriate video or CD to use during the lesson.

Lesson Objective

To teach the children that God has a job for them, just as he has a job for every person.

Opening Prayer

The same opening prayer is recited at the start of every class.

Circle Time

After God made Adam, He gave him a job to do. He wanted Adam to give a name to all the animals. Adam saw everything that God made, and really liked it. It was a big job to come up with all those names, and to remember them all. He worked hard and was proud of all those names.

God has a job for everybody. One of our jobs is to learn about God and to learn about His world. God is very happy when we work hard at these jobs.

Scripture Reading

Each aide should read the story of Adam naming the animals to their student from an ability-appropriate Bible.

Packet Work

It's time for the children to work individually (with their aide) on the goal-oriented work provided in the packet.

Group Activity

Make a zoo. There should be small stuffed animals or animal figurines around the room. Each child should have a few cards with the names of an animal on it. With their aide, each child should put the appropriate card beside the animals. When everyone is done, the class can take a tour of the zoo.

Video/Songs

Choose a thematically appropriate video, DVD, or selection of songs to play. During this time, the parents can meet for their Scripture study.

Closing Prayer

God help me do my job. Help me to learn about you and your world.

Note: Tell the parents to bring photos of family and friends next week.

Individual Reading

Read Genesis 2:4-20

Selected Scriptures

"The Lord God then took the man and settled him in the Garden of Eden, to cultivate and care for it."

GENESIS 2:15

"So the Lord God formed out of the ground various wild animals and various birds of the air, and brought them to the man to see what he would call them; whatever the man called each of them would be its name."

GENESIS 2:19

Contemplation

Even in the Garden of Eden, God had a job for man to do. People whose jobs have meaning and purpose have a contented heart and a joy that others lack. The job does not have to be a religious one; an individual's calling can be to be a doctor, a trash collector, or an administrative assistant. It is whatever we were made for. God has jobs for us to do. Those jobs are not just about lifetime careers. The jobs can be found in everyday life.

Our children have a purpose, too. Nicky, my nine-year-old son, is nonverbal, but he is the refiner of my soul. He has taught me more about patience, unconditional love, humility, and the redemptive side of suffering than any theologian ever could. So often as parents our capacity to love exceeds what we ever dreamed possible because of our children. Children challenge and transform the people around them to become better people. If that is not doing God's work, what is?

Discussion Questions

- Has your life found a new purpose since autism entered your family?

- How has having a child with autism affected your own spiritual development?

- What do you think God's plan for your child is for today and in the future?

Chapter 9

Adam and Eve
God Made Us for Others

CHILDREN'S CLASS

Materials and Preparation

- Pictures of family and friends
- A large picture of a tree with Adam and Eve at the bottom
- Baby names book for parents' study
- Rotate and add packet items as necessary. Choose an appropriate video or CD to use during the lesson.

Lesson Objective

To teach the children that we are all part of God's family.

Opening Prayer

The same opening prayer is recited at the start of every lesson.

Circle Time

Adam looked around and saw all the wonderful things that God had made, and he worked very hard at naming them all. He thought that God had done a very good job, but there was one problem—Adam was lonely. He wanted someone like himself to love and to share these things with. God understood, so He made a woman for Adam. Adam was so excited to have a friend, someone he could talk to and love. Adam named her "Eve." Together, they made man's first creation: a family.

We are made to be a part of families or groups of friends. We are all different, but we were made to love each other, just as God loves us.

Scripture Reading

Using an ability-appropriate Bible, each aide should read the story of Adam and Eve to their student.

Packet Work

Time to work individually (with their aide) on the goal-oriented work provided in the packet.

Group Activity

Make a "family and friends" tree. Have the kids come up and place their photos on a group tree, which has Adam and Eve at the bottom. After everyone's photos have been added, take a picture of it. Then let the students take their photos back to make their own tree to take home.

Video/Songs

Choose a thematically appropriate video, DVD, or selection of songs to play. During this time, the parents can meet for their Scripture study.

Closing Prayer

God, thank you for the friends and family that you have given me.

Individual Reading

Read Genesis 2:20-25 and 3:20

Selected Scripture

"The man called his wife Eve, because she became the mother of all the living."

Contemplation

In Scripture, names play a very important role. They not only identify the person, they often speak of their role in God's plan. Parents in biblical times often used the names of their children as a form of prayer to God. And God sometimes changed people's names at a momentous time in their life. *Abram* became *Abraham*, and *Sarai* became *Sarah*. In the Book of Ruth, Naomi changed her own name to *Marah*, which means "bitter." She wanted the world to know her sorrow over losing three sons.

I named my own sons Samuel *(of God)* Mark *(hammer),* and Nicholas *(people of victory)* David *(beloved).* I believe their names reflect their roles. In early times, hammers were used to shape metal into useful objects. My experience with my sons has transformed me into someone who can help bring victory in their lives. I owe it to God, my sons, and my own name, Kathryn *(pure)* Anne *(grace)*—which is what my name means.

Discussion Questions

- What does your child's name mean?
- Is there a particular reason that you picked that name?
- Can you see God's plan in that name?
- What does your name mean?
- If you could rename yourself, what would your name mean?

Chapter 10

Temptation
Sin Hurts, but God Always Loves Us

CHILDREN'S CLASS

Materials and Preparation

- Different kinds of fruit
- Individual bowls for the children
- Plastic spoons

For the group project, get bowls for the children to choose their own fruit for a fruit salad. Do not mix the fruit ahead of time; they can be picky eaters and may want all their fruits to be separate.

Rotate and add packet items as needed. Choose an appropriate video, DVD, or CD to use during the lesson.

Lesson Objective

To help the children understand that sin is God's name for things that hurt us.

Opening Prayer

The same opening prayer is recited at the start of every lesson.

Circle Time

Sometimes children do naughty things, like running into the street, even though parents and teachers tell them not to do that. Why is that dangerous? Well, if a car hits you, you could get very hurt and your parents and teachers want to keep you well. If you get hit by a car, your parents will still love you, but you will have to work very hard to get well again.

God tells us what to do, and what not to do, too. The things we do that can really hurt us or others, He calls "Sin." If we sin, we can hurt in many different ways. God will still love us, but He will have to work with us to get us back to being good.

God gave Adam and Eve all sorts of good fruits to eat in the Garden of Eden, but He told them there was one fruit that would be bad for them. Adam and Eve ate that bad fruit anyway. God was sad because Adam and Eve could not live in Eden anymore. Adam and Eve sinned, but He still loved them.

Scripture Reading

Each aide should read the story of Adam and Eve's sin to their student, using an ability-appropriate Bible.

Packet Work

It's time to work individually (with their aide) on the goal-oriented work provided in the packet.

Group Activity

Make a fruit salad. Set out bowls of fruit and have the kids make their own fruit salad in their own bowl. Some children may want only one kind of fruit in their "fruit salad." Make a fruit salad with all the remaining fruit for the children who are not as picky about what they eat. Say a prayer thanking God for all the good fruit He provides, and thanking the farmers who raise it.

Video/Songs

Choose a thematically appropriate video, DVD, or selection of songs to play. During this time, the parents can meet for their Scripture study.

Closing Prayer

God help me to tell when I have been naughty. Help me to do better and keep trying.

PARENT'S SCRIPTURE STUDY

Individual Reading

Read Genesis 3.

Selected Scriptures

"Then He asked, 'Who told you that you were naked? You have eaten, then, from the tree of which I had forbidden you to eat!' The man replied, 'The woman who you put here with me—she gave me fruit from the tree, and so I ate it.' The Lord God then asked the woman, 'Why did you do such a thing?' The woman answered, 'The serpent tricked me into it, so I ate it.'"

GENESIS 3:11-13

Contemplation

When things go wrong, it is human nature to look for someone to blame. We blame ourselves, others, God, or the devil. When it comes to autism, many parents carry a large burden of guilt. Others blame the environment or vaccines. If someone or something was at fault, then we believe that it was controllable.

We believe in the myth that we control what happens to us. To an extent, we do control what happens to us, because our actions have consequences. But there is much that we cannot control. We cannot control what other people do. We could not control when and where we were born. We could not control who our family was. Most of us cannot even control how much we eat. How reasonable is it to believe we could have controlled whether our child got autism? Many of us would rather feel guilty than out of control!

In the Bible, we see bad things do happen to good people. Sin entered here and will continue to wreak havoc. But we also see God enter into each of those situations and make it work for the good. We cannot control what happens to us. God does not force others to do what He wants them to do. But he can make any situation work out for our ultimate good.

We cannot know or control the future or change the past. But there is no cause for insecurity, because God was there and will be there. Most importantly, He is here now, making everything work out for our good. Free yourself from anxiety and forgive yourself and others. Embrace this, and soon you will find peace.

Discussion Questions

- Do you blame yourself for your child's condition?
- Do you blame your spouse?
- Who or what is your anger directed toward?
- Does blame or anger make your situation any better?

Chapter 11

Cain and Abel

Hurting Others Makes Things Worse

Materials and Preparation

- Food treats: donuts, cookies, and so forth
- Small toys—small balls, Slinkies, Playdoh, and Happy Meal toys. Make sure you have plenty of duplicates, in case several children want the same thing.

I don't recommend using the snacks from the group project snack tray during the Circle Time talk. The kids' attention will be focused on the snack and they will want it right away. For the group activity, the children will practice asking by word or by sign for what they want.

- Rotate or add packet items as needed.
- Choose an appropriate video, DVD, or songs to play.

Lesson Objective

To teach the children that asking for what you want is better than stealing or being angry.

Opening Prayer

The same opening prayer is recited at the start of every lesson.

Circle Time

Did you ever want a cookie that someone else had? If you grabbed the cookie, I'll bet you got a lot more than the cookie! You got everyone mad at you, too. And I'll bet you didn't even get the cookie! Someone probably took it away from you. Grabbing it probably made everything worse.

What should you do when you want a cookie that someone else has? You can ask your parents or teacher if you can have a cookie too. Did you know that we can ask God for the things we want or need? Sometimes he says "Yes," and sometimes He says, "No," and sometimes he says, "Later." The best times are when He says, "I have something better for you." If we learn to do things God's way, everyone is better off. Cain was mad at his brother Abel because he thought God liked Abel more. Cain did not ask God what he could do to make God happy. Cain got mad instead. Let's read to see what happened.

Scripture Reading

Using an ability-appropriate Bible, each aide should read to their student the story of Cain and Abel.

Packet Work

It's time for children to work individually (with their aide) on the goal-oriented work provided in the packet.

Group Activity

This is a project to help the children learn to ask for what they want. Have several treats or toys on a big plate. Have the kids ask for what they want through signing, pictures, or words. If they are able, have them ask God for what they want. Write those requests down and have them pray, "God, help." When we did this group project, my son asked for a white donut. Believe me, he got it.

Video/Songs

Choose a video, DVD, or a selection of songs to play. During this time, the parents can meet for their Scripture study.

Closing Prayer

God, help me to ask you for what I need. Help me share what I have.

PARENT'S SCRIPTURE STUDY

Individual Reading

Read Genesis 4:1-6

Selected Scripture

"...The Lord looked with favor on Abel and his offering, but on Cain and his offering He did not. Cain greatly resented this and was crestfallen."

GENESIS 4:4-5

Contemplation

It is hard for me when I encounter young children who are talking so effortlessly. I wonder how they can do that. My ten-year-old son still cannot talk. My thirteen-year-old has major issues with language. I grieve for my kids and for myself. It seems that life is not fair.

Cain, too, felt that life wasn't fair. He had a home, a good job farming the land, and a close relationship with God in which he could talk to Him directly. He counted these blessings as nothing because he did not have the favor that God placed on Abel's sacrifices. After Cain killed Abel, he lost all those blessings that he had taken for granted, and he wept. To make matters worse, Cain did not gain the favor in God's eyes that he had coveted.

47

When we look at the blessings that other people have, we can lose sight of what we ourselves have. We lose the enjoyment we could be getting from them.

When you envy others, you might as well have nothing, because that is the value you place on everything that is yours.

Discussion Questions

- What blessings do you have in your life?
- Do you view your child's autism as a punishment from God?
- Do you think God loves others more than you, because their children are healthy?
- Is your child with autism a blessing?

Chapter 12

Noah

God Finds a Way to Save Us

CHILDREN'S CLASS

Materials and Preparation

- Noah's Ark toy
- Some extra matching pairs of animals (as necessary) to provide at least one set for each student.

The Noah's Ark toy should be used for display during Circle Time. The same one is used later in the group project. For the group project each child will be given several pairs of animals to match and put on the ark.

Rotate and add packet items as necessary. Choose an appropriate video, DVD, or CD to use during the lesson.

Lesson Objective

To reassure the children that God is with us during times of change.

Opening Prayer

The same opening prayer is prayed at the start of every lesson.

Circle Time

Sometimes things change and it can be upsetting. Sometimes we might have to move or go to a new class. We are afraid because we do not know what will happen. But God is with us where we are now. He is with us when we are going through the changes, and He will be there in the new place. God finds a way to keep us safe with Him. Noah was a man who encountered big, scary changes. We'll hear about that when we all do our Bible reading.

Scripture Reading

Using an ability-appropriate Bible, each aide should read the story of Noah to their student.

Packet Time

It's time for the children to work individually (with their aide) on the goal-oriented work provided in the packet.

Group Activity

Provide each student with some matching animals to put on Noah's Ark. Students should take turns bringing their pair of animals to the ark.

Video/Songs

Choose a thematically appropriate video or selection of songs to play. During this time, the parents can meet for their Scripture study.

Closing Prayer

God, thank you for saving us when we are in trouble. Help us when we need to change.

Individual Reading

Read Genesis chapters 6 and 7.

Selected Scripture

"In the six hundredth year of Noah's life, on the seventeenth day of the second month, 'All the fountains of the great abyss burst forth, and floodgates of the sky were opened.' For forty days and forty nights, heavy rain poured down on the earth."

GENESIS 7:11

Contemplation

Do you remember the day you first heard the word *autism* in regard to your child? For most parents, that day is the beginning of the deluge. The days become a blur of worry, tears, and trying to find a cure. After a while, you get your feet underneath you again, but you find yourself in a whole new world. Everything has changed.

God is the ark that carries us through these changes. God's people are not spared the circumstances that affect others. We may be rocked and uncertain about the future, but we are able to endure. Later, we are able to overcome and build a new world for our families and others.

Discussion Questions

• What do you recall about the experience of learning that your child has autism?

• Are you still in the middle of the storm, or are your feet on solid ground?

• How has your world changed since autism entered your life?

• Where has God been in this process?

Chapter 13

Abraham
God Starts Many Nations

CHILDREN'S CLASS

Materials and Preparation

You can get the tune for the "Father Abraham" song at www.kididdles.com, and in many songbooks. The words have been changed to accommodate the abilities and sensitivities of children with autism.

Lesson Objective

To show the children that God can do great things with a person who loves him.

Opening Prayer

The same opening prayer is prayed at the start of every lesson.

Circle Time

Sometimes one man can have many children. These children then have children of their own, and it goes on and on throughout the years. That first father is called a patriarch. A patriarch of our faith is the first person to believe in God the way we do. Abraham is the father of many people and faiths. He had two sons: Isaac and Ishmael. Isaac is the father of all the Jewish people, and Ishmael became the father of many Arab people. Christianity was started by Jesus, who was a descendent of Abraham, so Christians call Abraham their father in faith.

You never know what great things God can do with one person who loves him and follows him. God can do great things with you, too, just as he did with Abraham.

Scripture Reading

Using an ability-appropriate Bible, each aide should read the story of Abraham to their student.

Packet Work

It is time for students to work individually (with their aide) on the goal-oriented work provided in the packet.

Group Activity

Gather the children together, in a circle if possible. This little song is sung to the tune of "Father Abraham." The original calls for the children to make arm and leg movements, which would be difficult for many of the kids. I have also made it more personal for the children by incorporating their names. Here's how it goes:

> Father Abraham had many kids
> Many kids had Father Abraham
> I am one of them, so is [child's name]
> So let's just praise the Lord.
> AMEN!

(Repeat for each child)

Video/Songs

Choose a thematically appropriate video, DVD, or selection of songs to play. During this time, the parents can meet for their Scripture study.

Closing Prayer

God, do great things with my life. I pray that what I do would being glory and honor to you.

PARENT'S SCRIPTURE STUDY

Individual Reading

Read Genesis 16, 17, 21:1 and 24.

Selected Scripture

"Sarah noticed the son whom Hagar the Egyptian had borne to Abraham playing with her son Isaac, so she demanded of Abraham, 'Drive out that slave and her son. No son of that slave is going to share the inheritance with my son Isaac.'" Abraham was greatly distressed, especially on account of his son Ishmael. But God said to Abraham, 'Do not be distressed about the boy or about your slave woman. Heed the demands of Sarah, no matter what she is asking of you, for it is through Isaac that descendants shall bear your name. As for the son of the slave woman, I will make a great nation of him also, since he too is your offspring.'"

GENESIS 21:9-13

Contemplation

Have you ever wished you could go back into the past and change a decision that you made? Sarah sure did. She did not have Abraham's faith that everything would work out the way God said. All she could see was her own inadequacy. She did not think that God could work through her, so she figured God would have to work through her servant. Sarah tried to make God's promise come true in her own way, and it blew up in her face pretty quickly. She lived with it grudgingly, until she saw that God had an entirely different plan—one that involved her. God was going to do for her what she could not accomplish on her own. Then she tried to get rid of Ishmael. He was messing things up for her.

God again had other plans. He loved Ishmael. He was Abraham's son too. He promised to bless him and make a great nation out of him. God loves us whether our parents planned for us or not, whether our parents wanted us or not. In the Bible, we see that many great people were born under questionable or difficult circumstances.

The truth is, if God did not use our stumbling and our poor efforts to follow him, he would have nothing to work with. He can do great things with whatever we bring Him, but He can do marvelous things when we obey Him and have faith.

When I look upon all the stress that autism has brought into my life, I can wonder what life would have been like if my son Nicky had never been conceived. But when he is happy and full of giggles, I think of all the joy I would have missed out on if he had never been born. I see what Nicky has done for my character development. I am more patient, kind, and non-judgmental than before. I don't know if autism is caused by man's mistakes with the environment, but I do know that Nicky is a gift from God, and that he was meant to be.

Discussion Questions

- Do you ever wonder what life would be like if your child with autism had never been conceived?

- What are some of the hardships you face with your child? (Do not share this in front of the children.)

- What are some of the joys?

Chapter 14

Isaac and Rebekah

Choosing Good Friends

Materials and Preparation

Develop a short script to depict several situations in which people act as friends or not as friends. You may want to include skits on cigarettes, drugs, and sexual abuse. Ask some of the aides to volunteer to perform in the skits.

Rotate and add packet items as needed. Choose an appropriate video, DVD, or CD to use during the lesson.

Lesson Objective

The objective of this lesson is to teach the children that good friends help them and that people who hurt them are not friends.

Opening Prayer

The same opening prayer is prayed at the start of every lesson

Circle Time

There are many people around us; some are good and some are bad. How can we tell if they would be good friends or not? Abraham's servant was given a job to find a good wife for Isaac.

He decided a good way to tell if someone was nice was to look at how they helped others. Not just how they help their friends, but also how they help strangers and animals.

This is a good way to tell if someone would be a good friend. Do they help others? Do they say nice things about other people? A friend would never tell us to do something wrong, or something that would hurt us. If someone tells you to do something wrong or dangerous, that person is not a friend.

The other thing Abraham's servant did was pray to God. He asked God to bring the right wife for Isaac to him. We need to pray that God sends the right friends into our lives.

Scripture Reading

Using an ability-appropriate Bible, each aide should read the story of Isaac and Rebekah to their student.

Packet Work

It's time for the students to work individually (with their aide) on the goal-oriented work provided in the packet.

Group Activity

Parents or other adults should act out different situations and ask the kids whether that person is being a friend or not. Be sure to portray a few scenarios for people acting like friends and for those not acting like friends. Friends could help someone up, or tell someone they are doing a good job. People who are not friends could offer someone else cigarettes or drugs or make fun of people. I strongly suggest that a skit about sexual abuse take place, because our kids are particularly vulnerable.

Video/Songs

Choose a thematically appropriate video, DVD, or selection of songs to play. During this time, the parents can meet for their Scripture study.

Closing Prayer

God, give us friends who bring us closer to you. Protect us from people who want to hurt us and who want us to do wrong.

PARENT'S SCRIPTURE STUDY

Individual Reading

Read Genesis 24.

Selected Scripture

"While I stand here at the spring and the daughters of the townspeople are coming out to draw water, if I say to a girl, 'Please lower your jug, so that I may drink," and she answers, 'Take a drink, and let me give water to your camels, too,' then let her be the one whom you have decided upon for your servant Isaac...."

GENESIS 24:13-14

Contemplation

Watching how someone treats strangers and animals is a good test of character. How you treat someone who cannot repay you is a show of an unselfish and hospitable heart.

Many parents of children with autism are single because autism can put a tremendous strain on a marriage. If you are single and looking for a new relationship, then observing how a person treats your child with autism can be a real window into that person's heart.

Stress can bring out the worst in people, or it can being out the best in them. If you react negatively to stress you can be irritable, angry, and emotionally overwrought. Stress leads some people to try to self-medicate with food, alcohol, or drugs. These responses are certainly human. With God's help, we can use these stresses to become kinder, less judgmental, more loving, and more patient. It is a long and difficult transformation process.

The best we can do is flawed, but flawed is okay. We cannot cure autism or change the minds of everyone around us, but we can love our child as he or she is.

Discussion Questions

- How do you react to stress?
- How does your spouse or ex-spouse react?
- What are some ways to relieve the stress on both of you?
- Do your expectations of yourself or your spouse add to the stress?

Chapter 15

Jacob
The Trickster

Materials and Preparation

- Poster board with picture of a ladder
- Rungs to place on the ladder
- Glue stick

For the group project, draw a ladder on a large piece of poster board. Write "God's Laws" on one side of the ladder, and "God's Prophets" on the other side.

Using construction paper, cut out several rungs for the students to place on the ladder. Each rung should be labeled with words like "prayer," "Reading Scripture," "Reading God's Word," "Doing what God says," and "Believing in God." Create and modify the rungs in a way that is significant to your faith's beliefs and practices. You should have at least one rung per child.

Lesson Objective

To show the children that there are many ways to get to God.

Opening Prayer

The same opening prayer is prayed at the start of every lesson.

Circle Time

Did you ever hit somebody only to have them hit you back? It hurt, didn't it? Jacob had a twin brother, Esau. Jacob tricked Esau out of his birthright and his father's blessing. Esau was very angry.

Jacob decided to go away to visit his uncle, Laban. You'll never guess what happened! Laban tricked Jacob into marrying both of his daughters. Now *Jacob* was angry. He had learned how it feels to be tricked out of something you worked hard for.

When Jacob went back home, he brought Esau many gifts to make up for tricking him. Esau forgave Jacob, and God blessed both of them.

When we hurt someone, we need to say we are sorry and try to make things right. God taught Jacob a lesson, and he teaches us lessons, too.

Scripture Reading

Using an ability-appropriate Bible, each aide should read the story of Jacob to their student.

Packet Work

Each child should work individually with his or her aide on the goal-oriented work provided in the packet.

Group Activity

On his way to see Laban, Jacob had a wonderful dream. He dreamed of a ladder going up to God. Today we are going to build a ladder. We are going to write the things that bring us closer to God on the steps of the ladder.

A ladder has two sides to hold it up. On one side, we have written "God's Law," and on the other side, "God's Prophets."

God's law is found in Scripture, where He tells us what to do. God's prophets are the people who tell us when we are not doing the right things.

(Have the children come forward one by one and add their rung to the ladder. Use a glue stick to attach the rungs.)

Okay. Now our ladder looks pretty good. But remember, a ladder cannot take you anywhere unless you climb it!

Video/Songs

Choose a thematically appropriate video, DVD, or selection of songs. During this time, parents can meet for their Scripture study.

Closing Prayer

God, help me to believe and to do good things.

PARENT'S SCRIPTURE STUDY

Individual Reading

Read Genesis 25:19 through Genesis 33.

Selected Scripture

"So, Isaac settled in Gerar. When the men of the place asked about his wife, he answered, "She is my sister." He was afraid that if he called her his wife, the men of the place would kill him on account of Rebekah, because she was very beautiful.

GENESIS 26:7

Contemplation

A woman I know sent out a Christmas card with her family members dressed in Christmas sweaters. What only her family knew was that her son with autism was wearing only the sweater—nothing else! She cropped the photo so it would be acceptable. When I heard this story, I thought it was very representative of the life of a family with autism.

As a mother of two boys with autism, I know how deep the desire is to be able to act like a typical family. Sometimes I am afraid of what people might think. Maybe they will think that I am a bad mother or, worse yet, abusing my child.

One night in a hotel room, my son became very agitated and started hitting his head and screaming. I knew what it must sound like on the other side of the wall. Fortunately, my son had gotten lost in the hotel earlier that day, so the staff knew what he was like. Neither the police nor Child Protective Services was ever called.

Jacob had fears, too. He was afraid to present his family the way it actually was. He also feared the very possible consequences. But he was not genuinely secure until the truth came out. Then the king was upset that Jacob had not told him about Rebekah.

I was secure in the hotel room only because the nature of my son's illness was known to others. Letting people into our lives can be painful, and it must done with some discretion. But as a family, we cannot feel loved and accepted as we are until people know us as we are.

The place to start is with other families with autism. They are the most likely people to understand. I would be cautious about people who are rigid and "by the book." Our lives seem to be written between the lines, or in the margins. Often, we figure things out as we go.

Discussion Questions

- Are you afraid to let people see you and your family as you are?
- How do you feel when people pass judgment on you?
- Do you assume that people are thinking the worst?
- Who is the worst critic of your parenting? You, or someone else?

Chapter 16

Joseph and His Dreams
God Has a Plan for Us

Materials and Preparation

- Multi-colored striped robe
- Several rolls of crepe paper, in different colors
- Rotate and add packet items as needed. Choose an appropriate video, DVD, or CD to use during the lesson

Lesson Objective

To help the children understand that God has a plan for every person's life

Opening Prayer

The same opening prayer is prayed at the start of every lesson.

Circle Time

Joseph was one of Jacob's sons. Jacob loved Joseph very much. Jacob gave Joseph a very special coat of many colors. But Joseph's brothers were angry because they didn't get a coat like that.

God loved Joseph very much too. He gave Joseph special dreams. Those dreams told Joseph that God had a special plan for him. Joseph's brothers were angry because they didn't get the kind of dreams that Joseph got.

Then Joseph's brothers did something very naughty. They sold Joseph as a slave to some people. They thought this would stop God's plan, but it didn't. God had a plan for Joseph's brothers, too. He just didn't tell them about it in a dream. They would have to live their lives first to find out about it.

God has a plan for your life, whether you know it or not. Just as with Joseph and his brothers, it is for good and great things. If we love God and try to follow him, other people will not be able to stop it.

Scripture Reading

Using an ability-appropriate Bible, each aide should read the story of Joseph and his family life to their student.

Packet Work

It's time to work individually (with your aide) on the goal-oriented work provided in the packet.

Group Activity

Use crepe paper to add colored stripes to everyone's clothes. Have as much fun as you want by encircling people with the crepe paper. Do whatever the children find fun.

Video/Songs

Choose a thematically appropriate video, DVD, or selection of songs. During this time, parents can meet for their Scripture study.

Closing Prayer

Thank you, God, for having a special plan for my life, even if I don't know what it is now.

PARENT'S SCRIPTURE STUDY

Individual Reading

Read Genesis 37.

Selected Scripture

"When his brothers saw that their father loved him [Joseph] the best of all his sons, they hated him so much that they would not even greet him."

GENESIS 37:4

Contemplation

It can hurt to be reminded of all you want and cannot have. Joseph's brothers wanted their father's love and approval and could not get it. When Joseph boasted of all the great things that were going to happen to him, it dug like a knife into his brothers' pain. They wanted to ignore his existence. Getting rid of Joseph would not win their father's approval, but they would not have to be reminded of it daily.

Hope can hurt. Sometimes when a new treatment or product comes along, you do not even want to hear about it. You've already been down that road, and it's ended in disappointment every time. So we try to kill that little voice inside us that wants to hope, and just be reconciled to how life is.

Despair is hope thrown down a well. Sometimes we're hurting on the inside, but we don't allow ourselves to hear it or truly feel it. If we allow hope and despair to speak, we will find they are the same part of us. Sometimes we put our hope in this treatment or that treatment, and when it fails, we lose our hope in God. This can happen when we think we're sure about the way God is going to work something out.

If we truly pour out our hopes, fears, and disappointments to God until we feel heard, then we can feel peace. We can accept when things don't go our way without despairing. When we know God has heard our cry, we will know that He is at work.

Discussion Questions

- Does it hurt to hope sometimes?
- Do you ever feel that God has let you down?
- Does it hurt you to see "typical" children?
- Do you feel too ashamed of these feelings to tell God about them?

Chapter 17

Joseph in Egypt
God's Plan is a Challenge

Materials and Preparation

- Cloth tunnels
- Large cardboard boxes
- Treats

Set up an obstacle course for the kids to go through. You can use cloth tunnels or cut open cardboard boxes for them to climb through. Have a treat ready for them at the end of the tunnel.

Rotate and add packet items as needed. Choose an appropriate video, DVD, or CD to use during the lesson.

Lesson Objective

To help the children understand that following God is not easy.

Opening Prayer

The same prayer is prayed at the start of every lesson.

Circle Time

Joseph had a really hard time in Egypt. Some people were very mean to him. They lied about him and even threw him in jail.

God made sure that there were also nice people around to help him. God never stopped loving Joseph. He got Joseph out of jail and left him in charge of the whole country. Joseph's brothers came and they were very sorry for hurting Joseph. Joseph forgave his brothers and they were able to live as a family again.

Sometimes people do mean things to us. God sees that, and someday he will make things right. We need to look for the nice people to help us during hard times. Turn the bad people over to God. Following God is hard, and forgiving people is even harder, but everyone benefits if we forgive.

Scripture Reading

Using an ability-appropriate Bible, each aide should read the story of Joseph in Egypt to their student.

Packet Work

It's time for the students to work individually with their aide on the goal-oriented work provided in the packet.

Group Activity

Set up an obstacle course for the kids to go through. You can have little cloth tunnels for them to crawl through, tables to crawl under, and chairs to climb over. At the end of the obstacle course, let there be a nice snack reward. Tell the kids that following God can be hard, but there is always a reward at the end.

Videos/Songs

Choose a thematically appropriate video, DVD, or selection of songs. During this time, parents can meet for their Scripture study.

Closing Prayer

God, help us to follow you and trust you even when life gets hard. Help us to forgive those who hurt us. Change their hearts so they can follow you too.

PARENT'S SCRIPTURE STUDY

Individual Reading

Read Genesis chapter 39 through chapter 45.

Selected Scripture

"He seized Joseph and threw him into the jail where the royal prisoners were confined. But even while he was in prison, the Lord remained with Joseph; He showed him kindness by making the chief jailer well disposed toward him.

GENESIS 39:20-21

Contemplation

Joseph reminds me of Job. Both were men who had horrible things happen to them. Job lost his family, his livelihood, his money, and his health. Joseph was also betrayed by his family, sold into slavery, falsely accused, and thrown into prison. Both, according to the Bible, were highly favored by God.

Many people think that if bad things happen to you, such as your child having autism, that you must have done something spiritually to deserve it. Job's friends thought that, and told him so often. Sometimes we tell ourselves that. The selected Scripture shows that God was with Joseph in his troubles, trying to make his life a little easier.

I believe one of the reasons God allowed Job and Joseph to suffer so much was that He knew all kinds of diseases, natural disasters, and other tragedies would befall people. He wanted them to know it did not mean that they had offended Him. It did not mean that He had turned His back on them.

Joseph and Job also show us that life can turn on a dime not only for bad, but also for good. Do not lose faith in God or feel that He has abandoned you or your family in your hour of need.

Discussion Questions

- Do you feel that you are being punished for something?

- Have you asked God for forgiveness?

- Guilt can make you feel unlovable. Do you feel that not even God could love you or forgive you?

- What evidence do you have that this is true?

Chapter 18

Moses in the Bulrushes

God Saves a Baby and the Future

Materials and Preparation

- A small plastic baby
- Numerous plastic Easter eggs or small boxes
- Treats to fill the eggs

Use the plastic baby to represent baby Moses during Circle Time. He should then be hidden in a box or an egg for the children to search for. For the group project, fill many small boxes or eggs with treats, including one with the baby Moses inside. Hide the boxes and have the children search for them. Have a meaningful prize for whoever finds baby Moses.

Rotate and add packet items as needed. Choose an appropriate video, DVD, or CD to use during the lesson.

Lesson Objective

To teach the children that following God helps those around them.

Circle Time

A Pharaoh was a leader of Egypt. Once there was a really mean Pharaoh. He was afraid of people who were different from him, and he tried to kill them—even the babies! Moses' mother loved him very much and did not want him to be killed. So she made a little basket and placed him into the water. She prayed that God would take care of him. God did! He sent Moses to the Pharaoh's daughter, who loved little Moses. Moses grew up to free all the Israelites, and to tell the world what God's law was. Moses changed the world forever.

When we place our lives and futures in God's hands and pray like Moses' mother did, God can do great things with us. We can change the world in little ways, or maybe big ways, just as Moses did.

Scripture Reading

Using an ability-appropriate Bible, each aide should read the story of Moses to their student.

Packet Time

It's time for the students to work individually (with their aide) on the goal-oriented work provided in the packet.

Group Activity

Have the children search for the baby Moses hidden in the eggs or boxes. Tell them they can keep all the treats they find, and that the one who finds baby Moses will get a special reward.

Videos/Songs

Choose a thematically appropriate video, DVD, or selection of songs. During this time, parents can meet for their Scripture study.

Closing Prayer

God, help us to keep searching for you until we find you.

PARENT'S SCRIPTURE STUDY

Individual Reading

Read Exodus 1 - 2:1-22

Selected Scripture

"When the child grew, she brought him to Pharaoh's daughter, who adopted him as her son and called him Moses; for she said, 'I drew him out of the water.'"

EXODUS 2:10

Contemplation

Moses' mother saved her son by giving him away. Because of the political situation, she knew she could not raise him herself. She had to trust God to guide her son to the right person. Pharaoh's daughter in turn entrusted Moses to his mother. She trusted that she would return him when the time came.

Parents of children with autism can have an interesting partnership with their children's teachers and school districts. We do not always have the emotional, financial, educational, or material resources to give our children the intensive education that they need. We send them off to school, hoping and praying that they will get the proper care.

We try to advocate for them, but everything involves dealing with another person to get the proper care for our children. Some parents end up home schooling their children. Many parents cannot home school, and many others would not want to even if they could. Sooner or later, we all reach the time when we must place our child in the basket and trust God for their care, first at school and, finally, at our death.

Discussion Questions

- Do you trust your child's teachers?
- How do you work out problems with them?
- Do you envision a time when your child can live apart from you?
- Are you working toward that goal?

Chapter 19

Moses and the Burning Bush

God Calls Us as We Are

Materials & Preparation

- Yellow and orange crepe paper
- Fan (make sure it's safe from little fingers)

During the group activity you will attach the crepe paper to the kids and have them walk in front of the fan, so they can look like a burning bush

Rotate and add packet items as needed. Choose an appropriate video, DVD, or CD to use during the lesson.

Lesson Objective

To reassure the children that we do not have to be perfect for God to use us.

Opening Prayer

The same opening prayer is prayed at the start of every lesson.

Circle Time

You might think that God wants to use the smartest people, or the strong, beautiful people, but God likes to use all kinds of people for his work—even people who think they're not smart or strong. Did you know that Moses had a hard time talking?

Here's what happened when God asked Moses to do something. God appeared to Moses in a burning bush. Moses was curious about the bush because it seemed to be on fire, but it wasn't burning up. God then spoke to Moses, and asked him to talk to the Pharaoh and the Israelites. Moses asked God to please ask someone else. "I have always had trouble talking," he said. He thought he talked really slowly and that everything he said came out sounding stupid. But God saw inside Moses' heart, and knew that Moses was the best person for such a big job.

Moses looked at what he could not do. God wanted Moses to look at what he could do with God's help. God let Moses bring his brother Aaron along to help him do the talking, but Moses was going to be God's miracle worker.

Everybody has problems. People do not need to be perfect for God to work with them. They need only have a good heart, and a willingness to follow Him.

Scripture Reading

Using an ability-appropriate Bible, each aide should read the story of Moses and the burning bush to their student.

Packet Time

It's time for students to work individually (with their aide) on the goal-oriented work provided in the packet.

Group Activity

Use orange and yellow crepe paper to cover the children with the fire of God's love. Have the children walk in front of the fan, so that the crepe paper will look like flames. Tell them that God's fire is different than regular fire. Regular fire burns and hurts people. God's fire doesn't burn bushes or people. Only God can make God's fire.

Video/Songs

Choose a thematically appropriate video, DVD, or selection of songs. During this time, parents can meet for their Scripture study.

Closing Prayer

God, set our hearts on fire with love of you. Help us serve you just the way we are.

PARENT'S SCRIPTURE STUDY

Individual Reading

Read Exodus 2:11 through 4:17.

Selected Scripture

"Moses, however, said to the Lord, 'If you please, I have never been eloquent, neither in the past, nor recently, now that you have spoken to your servant; but I am slow of speech and tongue.'"

EXODUS 4:10

Contemplation

Do you ever feel unequal to the task of parenting your child? You are in good company. Most parents of children with disabilities feel that way. Moses felt that way when God gave him a huge task to do. We prefer to feel competent, to know that we are equal to the task before us. That gives us self-confidence, but it doesn't provide growth.

God is like the ultimate coach—always pushing us to do more than we thought possible. After we start learning His ways, we start developing God-confidence and there is tremendous growth.

This growth is not just for ourselves, but also for all those around us. God did not push Moses just for Moses' sake; he did it for the sake of the Jewish people and all the people in the future.

When we pray, most of us usually ask God to help us accomplish our agenda. What we should pray is, "God, help us accomplish your agenda." Of course, this isn't as easy as it sounds. In practice, it's actually a lifetime of yielding our own hopes and dreams to God. It is willing ourselves to trust God even though we may feel hysterical or distraught. This way of life is as far above our ability to accomplish as freeing the Israelites was for Moses. The only way we can do this is through God doing it with us.

Discussion Questions

- What are your hopes and dreams for your child?
- What are your hopes and dreams for yourself?
- Do you think that God might have bigger plans for your family?
- How much control are you willing to yield to God?

Chapter 20

Moses and Pharoah

Standing Up for Your Beliefs

> ### CHILDREN'S CLASS

Materials and Preparation

- Ten "plague" finger-puppets (see Part One, Section D) or other symbols of the plagues

The finger puppets or other symbols of the plagues are used during Circle Time and during the group project. Find volunteers to perform the short skit of Moses and Pharaoh.

Rotate and add packet items as needed. Choose an appropriate video, DVD, or CD to use during the lesson.

Lesson Objective

To teach the children that not doing what God wants causes problems.

Opening Prayer

The same opening prayer is prayed at the start of every lesson.

Circle Time

Moses did what God asked him to do. He and Aaron together went before Pharaoh and asked him to let the Israelite people go. Pharaoh said no. So Moses showed Pharaoh some wonderful signs that God was with Moses, but Pharaoh still said no. Then God, through Moses, started sending plagues on Egypt. First, all the water turned into blood, but Pharaoh still said no.

Then, one by one, God sent eight more plagues: frogs, gnats, flies, a sickness that affected all the animals, boils on people's bodies, hail, locusts, and complete darkness. Pharaoh would not let the Israelites go. He said no, even though his people were crying. The Israelites were not hurt by these plagues because God protected them. The tenth plague was the worst. God took all the first-born boys. The people missed their boys and cried. Then, finally, Pharaoh said yes.

It is always better to say yes to God and obey Him. The more we sin and do wrong, the worse things get. God was going to save His people from this mean Pharaoh, no matter what it took. God will never stop trying to save us from evil. God also gives us chances to turn around and do what is right before sin destroys us.

Scripture Reading

Using an ability-appropriate Bible, each aide should read the story of the ten plagues to their student.

Packet Time

It's time for students to work individually (with their aide) on the goal-oriented work provided in the packet.

Group Activity

Today I am going to teach you a little song. For the adults, this is sung to the tune of "Louie, Louie."

Here's how the words go: "Pharaoh, Pharaoh, whoa, oh. Let my people go. Yeah, yeah, yeah, yeah, yeah, yeah, yeah."

Okay. Now I want you to sing it every time I ask you, "What did Moses say?"

Before we start singing, we need two adults to read the parts of Moses and Pharaoh.

Okay; are you ready? "What did Moses say?" (Kids and adults sing.)

Moses: "God says, 'Let my people go.'"

Pharaoh: "No."

Moses: "Then God will turn your water into blood."

Pharaoh: "Stop that. I'm sorry."

Moses: "God says, 'Let my people go.'"

Teacher: "What did Moses say?" (Kids and adults sing.)

Pharaoh: "No."

Moses: "Then God will give you too many frogs."

Pharaoh: "There are too many frogs. Stop it. I'm sorry."

Moses: "God says, 'Let my people go.'"

Teacher: "What did Moses say?" (Kids and adults sing.)

Pharaoh: "No."

Moses: "Then God will give you too many gnats."

Pharaoh: (swatting at gnats) "Stop these gnats. I'm sorry."

Moses: "God says, 'Let my people go.'"

Teacher: "What did Moses say?" (Kids and adults sing.)

Pharaoh: "No."

Moses: "Then God will give you too many flies."

Pharaoh: "Stop these flies; they are worse than the gnats. I'm sorry."

Moses: "God says, 'Let my people go.'"

Teacher: "What did Moses say?" (Kids and adults sing.)

Pharaoh: "No."

Moses: "Then God will make your animals sick."

Pharaoh: "Stop that! All my animals are sick. I'm sorry."

Moses: "God says, 'let my people go.'"

Teacher: "What did Moses say?" (Kids and adults sing.)

Pharaoh: "No."

Moses: "Then God will give you painful itchy spots all over your body."

Pharaoh: "Stop this itching. It is driving me crazy. I'm sorry."

Moses: "God says, 'Let my people go.'"

Teacher: "What did Moses say?" (Kids and adults sing)

Pharaoh: "No."

Moses: "Then God will send down hail that will damage your crops and hurt you."

Pharaoh: (avoiding "pretend" hail) "Stop that hail. It hurts. I'm sorry."

Moses: "God says, 'Let my people go.'"

Teacher: "What did Moses say?" (Kids and adults sing.)

Pharaoh: "No."

Moses: "Then God will send you locusts to eat all your plants."

Pharaoh: "Stop! The locusts ate all the food. I'm sorry."

Moses: "God says, 'Let my people go.'"

Teacher: "What did Moses say?" (Kids and adults sing.)

Pharaoh: "No."

Moses: "Then God will send you a darkness that will last three whole days."

Pharaoh: "Stop! I am so mad at YOU for making things so bad. Go away!"

Moses: "I will go away, but YOU have made things bad by not doing what God asked. He has one more plague. God will take your firstborn son, and then you shall cry and beg my people to go."

Next week, we will learn about what happened on the night of the last plague.

Video/Songs

Choose a thematically appropriate video, DVD, or selection of songs. During this time, parents can meet for their Scripture study.

Closing Prayer

God, help us to listen to you and obey you the first time you ask us to do something. Thank you for always trying to save us from evil.

PARENT'S SCRIPTURE STUDY

Individual Reading

Read Exodus 4:18-11

Selected Scripture

"But Pharaoh's servants said to him, 'How long must he be a menace to us? Let the men go to worship the Lord, their God. Do you not yet realize that Egypt is being destroyed?'"

EXODUS 10:7

Contemplation

Pharaoh was stubborn and Moses was steadfast. What was the difference between the two? The differences were in their attitudes toward God, themselves, and their people.

Moses was a humble man, well aware of his weaknesses. He allowed God to work through him, with the glory going to God. He was steadfast in what he did, not letting himself be intimidated by Pharaoh or by the Israelites when they grumbled. What he did benefited his people.

Pharaoh was an arrogant man, a god unto himself. He took advice from no one. He wanted all the glory and respect that men could give him. He would bend some when the going got tough, but then would snap back and change his mind. He was not there to serve his people's needs. The people were there to serve his needs.

These different leadership styles can be observed in families as well. A family is dysfunctional if only one member's needs are being met. This can happen when a child has a disability. Everyone's needs are not going to be met unless there is a conscious effort to fill them. This includes our own needs.

We are often swayed by the grumbling or wrath of others, but we must be careful not to let our children turn into little Pharaohs, calling all the shots. We need to stand firm, as Moses did, and not be intimidated. For their own good, our children need to learn that other people's needs are important too. We should teach them the joy that comes from helping others.

Under the leadership of Moses, the Israelites were led into safety. Under the leadership of Pharaoh, the Egyptians suffered greatly. Which leadership style will you choose for your family?

Discussion Questions

- Who best reflects your life right now? Pharaoh, Moses, the Egyptian servants, or the Israelites?
- Whose needs are met best in your family?
- Whose needs are met least?
- What would it take to make things more equitable?
- Can you stand up for what is right against arrogance or grumbling?

Chapter 21

Passover and the Red Sea

God Saves His People

Materials

- Certificates and awards
- Party supplies or Seder supplies

Have a party like the Israelites had on the shore of the Red Sea, or recreate a Seder. Give out certificates and awards to the kids. Rotate and add packet items as needed.

Lesson Objective

To celebrate that God saved us.

Opening Prayer

The same opening prayer is prayed at the start of every lesson.

Circle Time

Last time we talked about all the plagues that God sent on Egypt—all the plagues except the last one. Today I will tell you what happened with the last plague. Remember, God was going to take all of the firstborn boys. God told the Israelites, "I do not want you to cry. So take a lamb and put its blood on your doorway. I will see the blood and the plague will pass over your house and your kids will be safe." He also told them to eat some unleavened bread and some bitter herbs. He wanted them to be dressed and ready to go, because they would be leaving Egypt in the morning! So they all ate a big Passover meal and got ready to go.

The next morning, Pharaoh was very sad and angry. He told them all to leave Egypt, and so they did. But Pharaoh soon changed his mind again, and told his soldiers to bring the Israelites back.

Moses and the Israelites were up against the Red Sea, and Pharaoh's soldiers were behind them when God told Moses to stretch out his staff over the waters. The Red Sea opened up, making dry land for the Israelites to escape over. When the Egyptians tried to follow, the water flowed back. The Israelites were free!

God had saved them! Do you know what they did? They had a party because God helped them. So that is what we are going to do at the end of class.

Scripture Reading

Using an ability-appropriate Bible, each aide should read the story of the Israelites' escape to their student.

Packet Time

It's time for students to work individually (with their aide) on the goal-oriented work provided in the packet.

Group Activity

Party time! End-of-the-year party to celebrate God saving the Israelites and us. You can give out diplomas.

Closing Prayer

God, keep us safe and holy until we meet again.

Individual Reading

Read Exodus chapter 12 through chapter 15.

Selected Scripture

"They shall take some of its blood and apply it to the doorposts and lintel of every house in which they partake of the lamb. That same night they shall eat its roasted flesh with unleavened bread and bitter herbs."

Exodus 12:8-9

"But the blood will mark the houses where you are. Seeing the blood, I will pass over you; thus, when I strike the land of Egypt, no destructive blow will come upon you."

Exodus 12:13

Contemplation

God wanted to save the Israelites because they were his special people, and he loved them very much. When God says, "You are my people," He wants a response. He wants to hear "And you are my God." God made a covenant with Abraham and his descendants, and circumcision was to be the response.

On the night the plague came on the firstborn, God asked something more of the Israelites. He asked them to take a perfect lamb, sacrifice it, place its blood around their doors, and eat it up entirely, burning anything that was left. God also told them to make unleavened bread and bitter herbs. Their obedience to his requests would make the difference between life and death. On this night, the Israelites' response changed from, "and you are my God" to "and you are my God, my savior, and my Lord."

God also asked them to commemorate the Passover every year, and to teach their children to do so also. One of our most solemn duties as parents is to pass on our faith to the next generation. Your participation in this class has helped you do just that. It has been my privilege to help you.

Discussion Questions

- What is God calling you to do?
- How do you express, "and you are my God"?
- How have you and your children grown over the course of this Scripture study?

Resources

Children's Books & Other Materials

Children's books, teaching tools, and information about autism can be found in the following catalogs and websites:

Abilitations
800.850.8602

Autism-Asperger's Publishing Co.
913.897.1004 or visit *www.asperger.net*

Beyond Play
877.428.1244 or visit *www.beyondplay.com*

Different Roads to Learning
800.853.1057 or visit *www.difflearn.com*

Future Horizons, Inc.
800.489.0727 or visit *www.FHautism.com*

Jessica Kingsley Publications
011.442.078332301 or visit *www.jkp.com*

Mayer-Johnson Co.
800.588.4548 or visit *www.mayer-johnson.com*

Phat Art 4
866.250.9878 or visit *www.phatart4.com*

Pocket Full of Therapy
732.462.5888 or visit *www.pfot.com*

Special Needs Project
800.333.6867 or visit *www.specialneeds.com*

Super Duper Publications
800.277.8737 or visit *www.superduperinc.com*

The Center for Speech and Language Disorders
630.530.8551 or visit *www.csld.com*

Woodbine House
800.843.7323 or visit *www.woodbinehouse.com*

The ARC of the United States
301.565.3842 or visit *www.thearc.org*

Autism Research Institute
619.563.6840 or visit *www.autism.com*

Autism Society of America
800.3AUTISM or visit *www.autismsociety.org*

Doug Flutie Jr. Foundation
866.3AUTISM or visit *www.dougflutiejrfoundation.org*

Unlocking Autism
866.366.3361 or visit *www.unlockingautism.org/main.asp*

Index

D

E

F

About the Author

Kathy Labosh graduated from Penn State and became an economist. She is now a stay-at-home mom to Sam and Nicky, both of whom are children with autism. It became her mission to help others in similar situations. Kathy formed a Special Education Religion Class and is the author of a specialized curriculum for children with autism, currently in development.

Kathy continues to work on additional books in The Child with Autism series, including *The Child with Autism at Home and in the Community* (2011), *The Child with Autism Goes to Florida* (2011), and *The Child with Autism Learns MORE about Faith* (still in progress).

Ms. Labosh is also a speaker on the topic of autism. She spoke at the 2005 Catholic Educators conference, and has presented information to the Archdiocese of Philadelphia. She frequently speaks to groups near her home.

Kathy has also received an Honorable Mention for children's fiction from *Writer's Digest*.

Breinigsville, PA USA
22 February 2011
256153BV00001B/2/P